EVELYN UI

Anglican Mystic

Eight Letters of Evelyn Underhill

&

Essays by

A. M. Ramsey & A. M. Allchin

SLG Press
Convent of the Incarnation
Fairacres Oxford

ISBN 0 7283 0142 3
ISSN 0307-1405

Printed and bound by Will Print, Oxford, England

CONTENTS

Lawn House
12 Hampstead Sq.
N.W.3
May 3.1940

Dearest Daphne

I was so glad to get your letter & not at all surprised that you have been having a rough time with Convent theology. There always seems to be a time-lag in religious communities. They hang on to a religious outlook which the Church outside has dropped or transformed, or continue to use the pious language of the last generation. All this presses very hardly on educated subjects & probably causes the loss of many fine vocations. But it isn't so

Example of Evelyn Underhill's Handwriting

Foreword

In recent years there has been a remarkable revival of interest in the works of Evelyn Underhill. As sometimes happens in such things, it is the Americans who take the lead. When I went to the Underhill Celebration in the National Cathedral in Washington in March 1990, I was surprised to find how many of her books were in print, and delighted to discover that she had been included in the Calendar of the Prayer Book of the Episcopal Church. Since then her writings are again becoming more easily available in Britain; not only the big books like *Mysticism* and *Worship*, but also the books of retreat addresses and the volume of letters edited by Charles Williams. The continuing appeal of *Mysticism* is particularly striking. As Andrew Harvey, a contemporary writer on the subject, says, 'It still remains, after eighty years, the greatest book on mysticism I know.'

This pamphlet contains three things, all of which relate to Evelyn Underhill in the last and most creative period of her life. First there is a lecture given by Archbishop Michael Ramsey in 1975, during the commemoration of the centenary of her birth. This is followed by a lecture which I contributed to the Underhill Celebration. Finally there is a group of letters written by Evelyn Underhill in the last two years of her life to Daphne Martin-Hurst, a friend who had just entered the novitiate of the Community of St Mary the Virgin at Wantage. She and Evelyn had met in Daphne's first year as an undergraduate in Oxford in the early 1920s. The letters, with their wonderful mingling of wisdom affection and humour, give us a vivid glimpse into the mind and heart of this remarkable woman. Against the background of the fall of France, food rationing, repeated air raids on London and her own increasing ill health, the inner light of love and insight shines all the more brightly.

A. M. Allchin

Bangor, Wales
July 1996

Two Essays

The Mysticism of Evelyn Underhill

MICHAEL RAMSEY

We are commemorating the centenary of the birth of a personality remarkable in herself and remarkable also as a mirror of some great questions about the understanding of God, man and the world. A quaint episode in literary history focuses these questions as they emerged in Evelyn Underhill's life. She had published in 1911, when she was thirty-seven years old, a very learned and also very readable book with the title *Mysticism*. It sold well from the start, and its excellence was acclaimed by critics as different as Dean Inge and Dom John Chapman. However, an acquaintance, who was not at the time an intimate friend, wrote to say that he had not yet, as he had hoped, been able to make a thorough study of the whole work; but as a second printing of it was imminent he made two proposals, and he presented them in a tone just a little reminiscent of Hitler addressing the President of Czechoslovakia. I quote Baron von Hügel:

> 1) Either you rest content, so far as my little help is concerned, with these corrections proposed for the first four chapters—yet with the extension that you go through all the passages concerning *(a)* the supposed identity of man's soul and God, *(b)* the supposed non-necessity of institutional, historical, etc., religion for many or for some; and you would strictly weigh and reconsider them all, or,

> 2) you would get your publisher to defer the reprinting till the beginning of February, in which case I willingly undertake to give January to a careful study of your entire book.

Ruthless demands indeed! Either make some radical corrections or postpone the printing for a month—but it was advice as generous as it was peremptory. In fact, the book was reprinted in January with only a few alterations. But the penny had dropped, and in her later years Evelyn Underhill's energies were largely given to those questions which the Baron had posed so strongly. It is indeed those questions which will be in the foreground in this lecture, for I believe them to be as urgent as ever for a Christian understanding of the world.

I

Evelyn Underhill was born at Wolverhampton on 6 December 1875. Her father was a barrister, and the family was fairly well-off. Her education through her teens was mainly private, and later she went to the King's College for Women in London where she read history and botany. In 1907 she married Hubert Moore, a barrister. Before her marriage she had written novels and poems and had travelled much, with a special love for the natural beauty and the art of Italy; and she and her husband did a good deal of travelling in their early married life. But through the years her mind and imagination were stirred by mystical religion. The Church of England, which she had known from childhood, left her cold, not least for its lack of feeling for mysticism. Towards Rome she had strong leanings, and she and Hubert would often attend Roman Catholic services. Before their marriage it seemed very likely that she would be received as a convert. But there were causes for hesitation. Hubert vehemently disliked the idea of his wife becoming a Roman Catholic because he thought that to have a confessor might be a domestic barrier. Evelyn, anxious to persuade Hubert to a different mind, hoped that Father Robert Hugh Benson, convert, preacher and novelist, might soften Hubert's objections: after all, Benson was 'a decently educated English gentleman'. But a new hurdle appeared in the nick of time: the conflict between the Vatican and the Modernists about biblical criticism. Just after the wedding the Decree, *Lamentabili,* came with its censure of modernism, to be followed soon after by the more rigorous, *Pascendi Gregis*. Drawn towards Rome for its spirituality rather than its dogma, Evelyn recoiled before Rome's determination to suppress biblical scholarship. She never again came near to being a convert, though she and Hubert would still be found fairly often in Roman Catholic churches.

Mysticism was at the time her absorbing interest, and the book with that title embodied the studies of many years. What was, and is, the mysticism about which she wrote? I think it is important to distinguish two things. One is the historical phenomenon which she investigated with immense erudition and power of analysis. The other is her own interpretation of the phenomenon as a philosophy by which the world could be understood.

The phenomenon she investigated was a series of men and women, chiefly within the Christian tradition, who are commonly known as 'mystics'. They included St Augustine, St Bernard, St Catherine of Siena, the Lady Julian, Walter Hilton, St Teresa, St John of the Cross. The characteristic experience in virtue of which they are called mystics has been thus described by David Knowles in his book *The Mystical Tradition*:

> This knowledge, this experience...has three main characteristics. It is recognised by the person as something utterly different from and more real and adequate than all his previous knowledge and love of God. It is experienced as something at once immanent and received, something moving and filling the power of the mind and the soul. It is felt as taking place at a deeper level of personality than that on which the normal processes of thought and will take place, and the mystic is aware, both in himself and in others, of the soul, its qualities and of the divine presence and action within it, as something wholly distinct from the reasoning mind with its powers. Finally, the experience is wholly incommunicable, save as a bare statement, and in this respect all the utterances of the mystics are entirely inadequate as representations of the mystical experience; but it brings absolute certainty to the mind of the recipient.   (pp. 3f.)

This experience in its classic form has been known as 'passive contemplation'. Within the Christian tradition it has often been emphasised that the approach to this experience is not to have a desire for it but a desire to love and serve God. The passive reception of God's gift in the depths of the soul is of God's own gratuitous grace.

In her book, *Mysticism*, Evelyn Underhill analysed the factors in mystical experience in a psychological way with a remarkable thoroughness. But she did more. Using the word 'mystical' not only for the summit, but also for the foothills, and for many variants of the recognition of God in man and in nature, she set the mystics in the frame of a philosophy or total interpretation of the world and human life. In nature and in man there is a divine spirit whose essence is love, and through a response to divine spirit along the successive ways of purgation, illumination and union, the human self may come to be totally possessed by divine spirit and liberated to be its own true self, a soul of selfless love. Mysticism offers a philosophy of the world's true meaning. 'The world is one great stream of energy, characterised by thrust and effort; a struggle between matter and spirit, in which struggle becomes Act and energy is an internal push which has carried life by more and more complex forces to higher and higher destinies.'

This last sentence is not her own, for she never wrote such ugly prose. She is quoting from Bergson, on whom she relies for some of the steps in her thesis. The philosophical part of her thesis drew at least part of its material from him. But it was a thesis to which a number of contemporary streams contributed. One of the streams was a form of psychology described by Christopher Armstrong as 'the glamorous "science" of the pre-war period' (*Evelyn Underhill*, p. 112). Another is the concept of evolution, often used at the time as a kind of omnicompetent frame of reference. Another was the poetical kind of immanentism fashionable in much of the theology of the time. Not unfairly, Christopher Armstrong sees *Mysticism* as 'very much a book written "through a temperament", the temperament of a time and of an individual' (p. 126). There may be a touch of caricature in his description of this temperament as 'the effervescence of the cultivated classes of the Edwardian age', for though she lived in that atmosphere, Evelyn Underhill had her own intellectual rigour. Her creed was that 'the mystical life is not just a way of life some people fancy, but is truly the destiny of man, the crown and summit of all evolutionary processes'. She summed up the creed in lines at once clumsy and intense:

> Not to me
> The Unmoved Mover of philosophy
> And absolute still Sum of all that is,
> The God whom I adore: not this!

8

Nay, rather a great moving wave of bliss,
A surging torrent of dynamic love
In passionate swift career,
That down the sheer
And fathomless abyss
Of Being ever pours, his ecstasy to prove.

('Dynamic Love', in *Theophanies*, p.3)

Competent critics, themselves learned in the history of mysticism and untainted by the contemporary 'temperament', hailed *Mysticism* because it exposed the history of the subject with knowledge and scholarship. No book in English had come near to doing this in so massive a way. It was and is possible to learn from the book while being sceptical of the theory. But the theory continued, and the author presented it in the smaller work, *Practical Mysticism*, in 1914, having already applied the theory to the origins of Christianity in *The Mystic Way*, where the life of our Lord in the four Gospels is presented on the lines of a mystic's development. But a gentle voice was becoming audible in Evelyn Underhill's subconscious: 'Hearken, O daughter, and consider, incline thine ear'. We noticed earlier the Baron's demand for reconsideration. He had raised two issues: 'The supposed identity of the depths of man's soul with God. The supposed non-necessity of institutional, historical, etc. religions for many or for some'. These were matters on which he had pleaded for a thorough reconsideration.

II

She had once, as we saw, been very near to Rome. She thought there was a Rome of liturgy, other-worldliness and sanctity which appealed to her rather than a Rome of dogma and authority; but there is only one Rome, and she realised the one Rome was not her call. The question, however, which she was facing was not the merits of different Churches, but the place of history and historical institutions of any kind within true religion. The Baron could not proselytize, but equally he could not disown the claims of Rome. He was ready to help Evelyn towards a sense of the historical and institutional factors in Christianity along the path

9

she was able to follow. Indeed, the institutional question was subordinate to another question: is God to be identified with a diffused Spirit working in nature and in man; or is he the Creator upon whom his creatures utterly depend, and one who reveals himself in specific acts in history to set his creatures free for the way of living through dying? If the latter is true, and Evelyn Underhill was coming to believe that it was, then her massive knowledge of the mystics would not be wasted, but the path of her understanding of them would be different, as well as the path that her own spirituality would tread.

For my own part, I shrink from probing into the story of anyone's soul, even if the evidence seems available, and I am happier to see only where someone started and where someone arrived. This much, however, may properly be said: the intellectual movement in Evelyn Underhill which altered the shape of her theology seems to have synchronized with the needs of her own soul for a new kind of answer. Was it possible to go on living in the intense glow of feeling, thought and language which had been hers for a decade and more? Might it not be defeating its own meaning by a form of self-consciousness? Might not the doctrine of the duality of Creator and creature, on which the Baron had put his finger, offer her a freedom to find her own true self? Be that as it may, one chapter was ending and another was beginning.

It was from 1921 until his death in 1925 that Baron von Hügel was Evelyn Underhill's counsellor, and Margaret Cropper has shown in her biography, *Evelyn Underhill*, how the Baron helped her to understand what she had already begun to discover. 'Incarnation' is now the key noun, and 'incarnational' the adjective. The Baron writes to her about the ordered life of prayer, about liturgy and contemplation, about a width of practical relationships and activities: an incarnational spirituality. There is a doctrine beneath it. At an early stage he had written:

I fail to make sense of your frequentation of Holy Communion, even of Benediction, unless at the bottom of your mind there was an instinct, stronger than all mystical inclinations, that God does dwell in and manifest himself, by historical happenings, here more than there, now more than then...till we reach at last an apex of spirituality which is at bottom the deepest self-abasement of God in Jesus Christ in the manger and the Cross.

In another letter he writes of 'the factualness, happenedness of our Lord, especially the Passion and the Holy Communion.' For her part, she writes a little later:

As to Christocentric devotion I am still mainly theocentric, but the attitudes are no longer in opposition in my mind: they are two aspects of one thing. Now I have got my universe of one piece again...this has meant throwing overboard some Nicene language...but perhaps you will allow me a little latitude here?

We can be sure that the Baron would be ready to distinguish the intellectual formulation from God's unique presence and action in Jesus Christ, and that he would be no less sympathetic towards a critical attitude to the Gospels such as he had himself upheld in the Modernist controversy. So she wrote, 'The main historical happenings as given by New Testament criticism, and especially the Passion, are absolutely necessary to Christianity.'

So it was that Evelyn Underhill was seen from the nineteen-twenties onwards not as the exponent of mysticism or as an evolutionary philosopher, but as a doctor of the Christian Church. Perhaps the best exposition of the new trend of her thinking is found in *The Life of the Spirit and the Life of Today* and *Man and the Supernatural*. In these books much of the style and stress of the earlier books remains. But the frame of belief is different with the duality of Creator and creature, and the revelation of God in the Word-made-flesh always prominent. She is now the teacher, not only in her writings and in her work as a Fellow of King's College, London, but also in her retreats for clergy and laity, especially at Pleshey, near Chelmsford, and in many personal counsels. The sacramental aspect of her teaching is powerfully presented in *The Mystery of Sacrifice*, a work on the Eucharist which drew deeply from the spirituality of the Eastern Orthodox Church. Perhaps, however, the volume entitled *Worship*, in Nisbet's 'Library of Constructive Theology' (1936), best illustrates her latter-day style and method. Starting from a biblical foundation she traces the history of worship in the various forms of Christian tradition, drawing out the nature of worship as our response to God's action as Creator and Redeemer.

III

The book *Mysticism* appeared in a fourth and much-revised edition in 1930, with an important new Preface. In this she describes what she calls a transformation in the study of mysticism, not only in England, but in France, Germany and Italy, since the book was first published. One change is that study has disentangled mysticism as man's essential religious experience from the psycho-physical accessories which sometimes accompany it, so that 'no responsible student now identifies the mystical and the ecstatic, or looks upon visionary and other extraordinary phenomena as either guaranteeing or discrediting the witness of the mystical saints.' We are now, she says, 'more able, thanks to the criticisms of the psychoanalytic school, to distinguish the genuine spiritual activities of the psyche, while explaining in a materialistic sense some of their less fortunate physical accompaniments.' The other change which she saw was in the philosophical and theological landscape. In this there had come a new friendliness to transcendence and the concept of the supernatural. It was indeed a change from the pre-1914 liberalism to the theological world of Rudolph Otto, Karl Barth, the Thomist revival, the beginnings of Neo-Orthodoxy and the heyday of Anglican sacramental devotion. Against this background of change she considers how the book might be different if she were now writing it for the first time, and she writes these significant words:

Though the mystic life means organic growth its first term must be sought in ontology, in the vision of the Principle, as St Gregory the Great taught long ago. For the real sanction of that life does not enter in the fugitive experience or even the fecundity of the subject, but in the metaphysical object which the subject apprehends.

Baron von Hügel died in 1925. In the succeeding years Evelyn Underhill became known as one whose teaching conveyed much of his thought. While guiding others, she was herself guided first by Bishop Walter Frere and later by Reginald Somerset Ward. She did much to extend the tradition of 'spiritual direction' which elicits people's own spiritual capacities and helps them to find themselves in paths of freedom. She died in 1941. In retrospect we may see her as far more than an echo of the Baron. She was able to use the insights she had gained from him and from her own studies for the expression of a theology and spirituality of a distinctively Anglican kind. Few in modern times have done more to show the theological foundations of the life of prayer and to witness to the interpenetration of prayer and theology. She has a place of her own, and it is an important one.

IV

Since Evelyn Underhill's death the changes in the world, in religion, in theology and in philosophy have been greater by far than those which happened in her lifetime. In Western Christendom there has been the period when the quest for God within the secular has been strong, with the emphasis upon social activism and the impatience with religious practice. But this phase has in turn been followed by a revival of religious hunger in many forms, Christian and non-Christian, intelligent and fantastic. As there had been in Western Christendom a long and tragic neglect of our own Christian mystical tradition it is not surprising that the spiritual hunger causes many to look towards the mystical practice of Eastern religions. Indeed, the greater involvement of continents, peoples and religions with one another has made this openness to the lessons of other faiths inevitable. Evelyn Underhill's writings, however, do not give much direct guidance in this field, for in spite of her feeling for Eastern Orthodox spirituality, and her friendship with Rabindranath Tagore, her studies were devoted to the mysticism of the Christian West.

Today the investigation of mysticism calls for a wider field of East and West than Evelyn Underhill was able to compass. For such investigation it seems that there are some facts and principles about the relation between Christianity and mysticism which are inherent in the nature of Christianity itself. I would dare to end by suggesting what some of these facts and principles may be.

The Christian way, as known and expounded in the New Testament writings, is not to be defined in terms of mystical experience. It is a way of union with God in Christ through faith, issuing in love and hope. 'It does not yet appear what we shall be.' Living *in via* and not yet *in patria* Christians receive through the Holy Spirit anticipations of their heavenly goal. One of these anticipations, given to some, is the mystical experience known as 'passive contemplation', when the soul knows itself to be possessed by God to the depth of its existence. That such experiences should happen is a source of encouragement and joy to those who receive them , and to other Christians. But it is not by such experiences that the Christian way is defined, for it is defined by that which is the privilege of all Christians, the response of faith and love in all the variety of its stages and its gifts. Let it again be emphasised that the Christian mystic does not long for experiences; he longs to love and serve God, and the outcome of mystic experiences is not a desire for their repetition, but an enhanced desire to do the will of God. The relation between mysticism and Christianity rests upon the right understanding of both.

It may, therefore, make for understanding if Christians practice restraint in the use of the word 'mysticism', and employ it to describe the distinctive experience of 'passive contemplation', rather than contemplation in general or prayer in general, though the adjective 'mystical' is likely to be used more widely to describe the experiential aspect of religions. Should we not, in any case, avoid the distinction sometimes made between 'acquired' contemplation and 'infused' contemplation, as if we could climb the foothills by our own efforts and needed God's grace for the higher ranges? All is God's gift, whether the mystical experience of a St John of the Cross, or that kind of contemplation of God which is accessible to all those who want to want God, however feeble their wanting may be. All is of God; no one can be nearer to God than the man in the parable who said, 'God be merciful to me, a sinner', or the robber who cried on a cross on Calvary, 'Jesus, remember me when you come into your kingdom.'

Evelyn Underhill and Anglican Spirituality

A. M. ALLCHIN

In the chapter on 'The Anglican Tradition' in her great book *Worship*, published in 1936, Evelyn Underhill describes some of the promising developments which she saw in the Church of England at that time. 'The new life,' she writes, ' is specially seen in Cathedrals; once they were little better than badly kept museums where the spirit of prayer was firmly discouraged.' A footnote reads, 'Young woman,' said the pre-war verger of a great cathedral to a visitor caught reading her New Testament, 'only guide books may be read here.' Now she asserts that though much remains to be done, the cathedrals are beginning to be recognised as places of prayer and worship the mother church of the diocese.[1] She was always concerned that prayer and worship should be at the very heart of the Church's life.

In this article I intend to think of the mature Evelyn Underhill, the woman who in the last twenty years of her life became known as a writer, a teacher, a director, a conductor of retreats, and thus became in herself a leading exponent of Anglican spirituality. I shall not speak much of Evelyn's direct influence on others; that will be implied in much that I say. Nor shall I speak about her constant care to link spiritual with social concerns, not to allow the inner life to become divorced from our outer life of public responsibilities. If I have neglected this very important aspect of her teaching, in which she shows herself altogether true to the Anglican tradition, it is in part because others have already taken it up and expounded it powerfully. I think of the writings of Dana Greene in the United States, above all her biography, *Evelyn Underhill, Artist of the Infinite Life* (1991); and of Terry Tastard's brief but substantial essay in his book *The Spark in the Soul* (1990).

It must be now more than forty years since I first came across the writings of Evelyn Underhill. While I was still at school I was given a copy of the selection of her letters edited by Charles Williams. It was book which fascinated me and influenced me greatly. On the one side it opened up a whole world of spiritual writings, Ruysbroeck, Richard Rolle, St John of the Cross, St Francis de Sales, which had previously been almost wholly unknown to me. On the other side it brought this somewhat exotic world of mystical experience remarkably close. The letters were written in a practical, down-to-earth way with more than a dash of humour, and gazing out from the photograph which faced the title page was an elderly lady looking rather like one of the older members of my own family.

Since that first contact with Evelyn Underhill's writing, there have come to me, over the years, a number of meetings with people who had known her rather well personally.[2] From them I have gained a fairly clear impression of how she appeared to her friends in the last fifteen or twenty years of her life. Part of her secret, part of her disguise, if you like, was her outward ordinariness. She didn't look anyone outstanding. On the first occasion when she intervened in a meeting of the Fellowship of St Alban and St Sergius, the noted Russian theologian, Father Sergei Bulgakov, came at the end of the session to ask the Secretary, Nicholas Zernov, 'Whoever is that little woman? She knows far too much.' I suspect that he had observed that she knew a great deal too much not only at the level of academic study, but also at the level of personal experience. For whatever reason, she was someone who made a very powerful impression on the Russian Orthodox.

Outwardly she was ordinary. Her piety was deep but it was also reticent. She was a woman of great intellectual capacity and spiritual understanding, but she did not normally allow that to appear on the surface. What you saw immediately was a charming, witty, vivacious person with a sharp sense of humour, which could easily have become too sharp if it had not been held in check by her kindliness and deeply-rooted charity. She and her husband were people who appreciated good conversation; it sccms to have been something of an art at their table. She was a person of varied interests, but utterly without pomposity or pretension. The only people she found really difficult were gushing, sentimental admirers who made too open a display of their piety.

In this outward reticence we have a quality which was typical of the time and the society in which she lived. Deep feelings were discussed and analysed much less than in our psychologically over-articulate world; they were not easily revealed. A letter which Evelyn wrote in 1910 to her friend Margaret Robinson is interesting in this regard. She is discussing the question of how to behave when visiting a church with people who know nothing of what it is or means:

> I certainly would not in any company pass an altar of the Blessed Sacrament without kneeling; but apart from this, I really think there is something to be said in favour of varying one's practice according to one's company. After all, the object of kneeling down is to pray—and it is not easy to do that under the amazed eyes of one's fellow creatures! I think there is a legitimate reserve and shyness in religion which is not cowardice any more than refusing to kiss anyone you love in public would be cowardice.[3]

It is good to be reminded how much our most simple conventions of behaviour have changed in the course of the last eighty years.

On this subject of reticence and shyness it is interesting to note that though Evelyn and her future husband had known each other since their adolescence, it was more than twelve years before they began as she says, 'to talk openly about all the real things which we sedulously kept from each other'. That was in 1907, shortly before their marriage. In later life we see them as a couple who had many things in common, but who in certain vital areas of their life seem to have had little to say to one another. They loved their sailing holidays together; both were fascinated by craft work (book-binding for Evelyn, metal-work for Hubert); they shared a wide circle of friends, legal and literary, their families had long been in contact with one another. But their marriage seems to us so quiet and unemphatic, that there are some who are inclined to have doubts about its nature. For myself I must say that all that I have heard from those who knew them suggests that, granted its limitations, it was in many ways a surprisingly good marriage. Evelyn did not enter into Hubert's professional world, nor would anyone have expected her to do so. Hubert did not enter into hers; that would have been equally unacceptable.

However, they supported each other in their whole life-work, and in a note written by Evelyn to a younger friend, Agatha Norman, we have a glimpse of them together which reveals a kind of intimacy which is usually hidden from us. They were listening together to the wireless, to a broadcast review of Evelyn's recently published *Worship*. It was evidently a highly favourable review, and Evelyn tells us that Hubert kept looking into her face to see if she was blushing. It is clear that her marriage provided her with a secure base from which she could undertake her many-sided work. It provided a solid place to which to return.

To some of Hubert's friends, it must be admitted, her activities were of very little significance. I remember meeting a retired military man in Oxford in the early sixties, and discovering that he had known Hubert Stuart Moore as a sailing companion, I said with perhaps naïve enthusiasm, 'How wonderful to have known Evelyn Underhill's husband!' My interlocutor was clearly puzzled by this remark, and when I explained that Hubert's wife had been a quite well-known author, 'Oh yes,' he replied, 'I believe she did write books or something. It was a trouble to Hubert, but he was very good about it.' Despite such remarks, I have the impression that Hubert was less uninterested in her writing than many have supposed. Certainly he acted as a kind of agent for her, keeping accounts of royalties and new editions. It was he who edited the first of her posthumous works, *The Fruits of the Spirit*, in 1942.

Clearly Evelyn was careful not to embarrass her husband by parading her own successes or her own special interests. She took care of him in this as in all things. Agatha Norman has told me how she had a rather pressing invitation to Sunday afternoon tea during the later thirties. She was invited so that Hubert should not be left without conversation while Evelyn was engaged on the other side of the room with another regular Sunday visitor with whom she had much in common. His name was T. S. Eliot. In

Margaret Cropper's biography there is another interesting glimpse of her desire not burden Hubert with her own particular work:

> Dorothy Swayne remembers how once when she was staying the night at Campden Hill Square, Evelyn switched off their intimate religious talk to welcome Hubert as he came in from work; and how natural it all seemed when Hubert enquired, 'And now, Miss Swayne, what would you like to drink?'[4]

The hospitality of their house was not restricted to their particular friends. Every Christmas Eve they kept Open House for the other residents in their square for what Evelyn called, 'the party of the three C's,' carols, candles and cakes. For years after her death the custom was maintained of every house in the square putting lighted candles in their windows on that day. It was a custom which had been begun by the Stuart Moores.

I have spoken at some length of the ordinariness of Evelyn Underhill, and in particular of the ordinariness of her marriage. But that ordinariness was, of course, only on the surface. Inwardly she was anything but ordinary. Here was a person of immense intellectual energy—consider the volume of her publications. Here was a person of profound spiritual insight—consider the extent of her influence. W. R. Matthews, first Dean of King's College, London, and then Dean of St Paul's Cathedral, couples her name with von Hügel's as a guide in spiritual matters: 'Baron von Hügel and Dr Evelyn Underhill were probably the two most powerful personal spiritual directors for educated persons in their generation.'[5]

But it was this outward ordinariness which was responsible in part for her remarkable achievement. One of the extraordinary facts abut Evelyn Underhill was the way in which she was able to break through so many barriers, without apparently arousing controversy or vocal opposition. The first woman to lecture in the Theology Faculty in Oxford, the first woman to establish her position as a retreat conductor, the first laywoman to have been widely recognised in the Church of England as a spiritual director. The only comparable figure in the nineteenth century would have been Mother Harriet Monsell, the first Superior of the

Community of St John the Baptist at Clewer, whose influence spread far beyond the boundaries of her own community.

How was all this done? It was done partly, at least, through Evelyn's willingness to act in a totally unofficial and personal capacity. With the single exception of her honorary Fellowship at King's College, London, she was attached to no centre, no institute, no foundation, academic or ecclesiastical. In a letter of 1932 she writes, 'it is one of the advantages of being a scamp, that one in unable to crystallize into the official shape, and so retains touch with other free lances, and realizes how awful the ecclesiastical attitude and atmosphere often makes them feel.'[6] She was free of the establishment, not crystallized into any official shape. She was simply Mrs Stuart Moore, writing her books and seeing her friends from her modest but beautiful house in Campden Hill Square. The disguise had its ecclesiastical uses, as well as its more intimately spiritual ones. It enabled her to keep in touch with many others who, like herself in earlier life, had been unable to come to terms with the institutional Church. It enabled her to break down barriers without frightening people too much.

Though still freelance, by 1932 Evelyn had been firmly rooted in her ecclesiastical allegiance for over a decade. Since the circumstances in which, in the years after the First World War, she decided to become a practising Anglican are not very clear, it may be useful to consider what actually happened. Let us hear her own account of her first approach to Catholicism. In a letter written in 1911 she tells a friend how, early in 1907 she had been converted,

> quite suddenly, once and for all, by an overpowering vision which had really no specific Christian elements, but yet convinced me that the Catholic religion was true. It was so tightly bound up with (Roman) Catholicism, that I had no doubt and have had none since...that that Church was my ultimate home. So strong is this conviction that to have any personal dealings with Anglicanism seems to me a kind of treachery. Unfortunately I allowed myself to be persuaded to wait a year before being received; and meanwhile the Modernist storm broke, with the result that now, being myself 'Modernist' in many points, I can't get in without

suppressions and evasions to which I can't quite bring myself. But I can't accept Anglicanism instead; it seems an integrally different thing. So here I am, going to Mass and so on, of course, but entirely deprived of the sacraments.[7]

This conviction of the truth of the Catholic religion was not something which altered over the years. What did alter was her estimate of Anglicanism. She found that to commit herself to the Church of England, even if at first reluctantly, was not an act of treachery to her vision. She no longer conceived of it as 'an integrally different thing'. She found it to be part of the Catholic whole. Like T. S. Eliot, she found in the communion of that Church a way of being Catholic, an authentic and life-giving way, though not without its own perplexities. So, in a letter written in 1931, a decade after her return to the church of her upbringing, she writes to Dom John Chapman, the abbot of a leading Roman Catholic monastery:

I have been for years now a practising Anglo-Catholic…and solidly believe in the Catholic status of the Anglican Church, as to orders and sacraments, little as I appreciate many of the things done among us. It seems to me a respectable suburb of the city of God—but all the same, part of 'greater London'.[8]

II

If we want to see more of what Evelyn meant by this letter, and how in her later years she understood the Catholicism she had embraced, we can best do so by referring to her volume, *Worship*. But before we do that, let us turn back to the letter of 1911, in which she had expressed her longing to be united with Rome. Her feelings at that moment were mixed, for apart from the theological issues raised by the modernist crisis, her way towards Rome was also blocked by the rigidity and exclusiveness of Roman Catholicism as she saw it at that time in England. She wrote to her Anglican correspondent:

I no more like the tone and temper of contemporary Romanism than you do: it is really horrible; but with all her muddles, she *has* kept her mysteries intact. There I can touch—see—feel Reality: and—speaking for myself only—nowhere else…The narrow exclusiveness of Rome is dreadful—I could never believe it, for I feel in sympathy with every Christian of every sort—except when they start hating one another.[9]

It is interesting to find these words about her feeling of sympathy for all her fellow Christians directly echoed a quarter of a century later in the preface to *Worship*. There she tells us that she had been criticised for this very thing:

Some of the friends and fellow-students who have read these chapters have been inclined to blame me for giving too sympathetic and uncritical an account of types of worship which were not their own. It has been pointed out to me that I have failed to denounce the shortcomings of Judaism with Christian thoroughness, that I have left almost unnoticed primitive and superstitious elements which survive in Catholic and Orthodox worship, that I have not emphasized as I should the liturgical and sacramental shortcomings of the Protestant sects.[10]

To have done this, she says, would have been easy. Nothing is simpler than to denounce the negative elements in another person's position. But it would be ultimately fruitless, for people do not normally live off their negations. They live on the affirmations which they make in life, in worship and in doctrine. If we want to understand them we must seek to sympathise with what they affirm.

So the kind of Catholicism to which she aspires, which we see reflected in *Worship*, is a kind of Catholicism which has much more in common with Vatican II than with Vatican I. It opens itself to all that is true and good, wherever it is found. It is prepared to find it in unexpected and very varied places. *Worship* formed part of a series called 'The Library of Constructive Theology', whose general editors were two well-known liberal theologians, the Anglican, W. R. Matthews, and the Non-conformist, H. Wheeler Robinson. The presence of her book in this series reveals that she was clearly aware that her Catholicism had something of a liberal character particularly in this matter of ecumenical openness. In this respect her attitude differed widely from the aggressive triumphalist style of much Anglo-Catholicism in this inter-war period. Her contacts with the Anglo-Catholic Congresses, which represented that tendency at its most militant, seem to have been slight. Like von Hügel, Evelyn rejected some of the basic dogmatic positions of the Catholic Modernists. The theological position taken in *Worship* in 1936 is far more balanced and traditional than is the viewpoint reflected in *Mysticism* twenty-five years before. But she never repudiated the liberal virtues of openness of mind, the liberal respect for the findings of critical scholarship, and a desire to relate the faith to the questions raised by developments in the world of her time. We find in her writings a liberality of method and approach rather than a liberalism of conclusions.

Dean Matthews, who had the major role in commissioning the book, was anxious in case she did not do justice to the more Protestant traditions of worship. He was afraid that she would concentrate too much upon the Catholic centre. Judging from the book as we have it, we may say that his fears were unnecessary. The chapter on 'Reformed Worship', in which she includes the classical Prostestantism of Scotland and continental Europe, both Lutheran and Calvinist, is a careful survey of its subject. In the chapter headed 'Free Church Worship', she follows through the traditions which have taken their origins in the Anglo-Saxon world, Baptist, Congregationalist, Methodist and Quaker. She is, like all of us, to some extent limited by her own experiences and her own sympathies. Holidays spent in Norway allowed her to give a vivid, firsthand account of the Sunday worship in a little village church in that most Lutheran of countries; but her treatment of the Lutheran tradition as a whole is one of the least satisfactory parts of the book. On the other hand, her evident sympathy with the Society of Friends, enabled her to describe their way of silent prayer with special inwardness and understanding.

At times in these pages she seems to catch fire. This is the case, for instance, when she comes to the hymns of Charles Wesley:

Like all the greatest creations of Christian devotional genius, they are both theological and personal; charged with dogma, yet so penetrated by the spirit of adoring and confident love that the firm outlines of the doctrinal framework are not at first observed.

In a footnote she instances a number of well-known hymns, among them 'Love Divine, all loves excelling,' and 'O, Thou who camest from above':

This doctrinal framework is seen on examination to imply so rich and deep a conception of the Godward life of man, that it requires for its full explication all the complementary aspects of Christian and Catholic worship; the expressive and sacramental, no less than the personal and interior.[11]

These last words are worth dwelling on. Her vision of Christian worship is by no means simply eclectic. She does not pick things at random here and there. She has a vision of a fullness and a balance of Christian truth and worship, an underlying Catholic structure, centring on the mysteries of the Trinity and the Incarnation, which does not exclude the complementary affirmations of the evangelical traditions, but includes them in a larger, deeper whole. This becomes clear in the two fine chapters devoted to the Eucharist and in the chapter headed 'Catholic Worship, Western and Eastern'. Note that the Eastern Orthodox element has here entered into the centre of the picture, and is joined to that beloved Latin tradition through which she had first glimpsed the splendour of Christian worship in its fullness. Through her membership of the Fellowship of St Alban and St Sergius she had come into a living contact not only with the theology of the Russian emigration, but also with its deeply-felt liturgical faith and piety.

The Fellowship was a body which she found unexpectedly congenial. Founded in the late 1920s by members of the British and Russian Student Christian Movements, it was predominantly, but never exclusively, Anglican and Orthodox. Methodists and Presbyterians had been among its first members. It was one of the rare places in Britain before Vatican II where Roman Catholics were able to meet their fellow Christians in friendly dialogue.

From the beginning it had placed eucharistic worship, though without intercommunion, at the heart of its life. Each day at a Fellowship conference the Eucharist was celebrated in alternating rites, Eastern and Western, as it still is. At the time when Evelyn Underhill was active in its life in the middle years of the 1930s the outstanding personalities at its meetings were Fr Sergei Bulgakov on the one side, and Bishop Walter Frere, Evelyn's friend and spiritual counsellor, on the other. It was a privileged moment of mutual discovery and mutual interrogation, in which Fr Sergei made his prophetic but unheeded proposal for a limited sharing in the Eucharist itself.

These Orthodox contacts touched Evelyn Underhill in a variety of ways. One of the most striking of her published letters is dated 30 June 1935:

> This morning was so queer. A very grimy and sordid Presbyterian mission hall in a mews over a garage, where the Russians are allowed once a fortnight to have the Liturgy. A very stage property Ikonostasis and a few modern Ikons. A dirty floor to kneel on and a form along the wall...And in this two superb old priests and a deacon, clouds of incense, and at the Anaphora, an overwhelming, supernatural impression.[12]

As we read the sections in *Worship* which deal with the prayer of the Orthodox Church, we can hardly fail to find passages of outstanding quality. This is not only, nor even primarily, the case with the account of the eucharistic liturgy itself, but also with her discussion of the nature of personal prayer and its place within the life of the whole worshipping community. In this passage I believe she writes not only out of her insight into Orthodoxy, but also out of her own experience within Anglicanism, an experience which perhaps her Orthodox contacts had helped her to articulate:

> A great reserve and a great freedom characterize the personal life of prayer in Orthodoxy; and for this reason it is difficult to form any clear conception of it. Eastern Catholicism is penetrated by the conviction that the true Object of its worship transcends all definitions. That which any one soul can apprehend is only a fragment; yet this fragment

implies the whole mystery of that which we adore. Therefore within the total Godward life of the Church to which the Divine Liturgy gives ritual form, it is ready to allow great liberty of response to individual souls. There is something here for all levels and types, from the most naive to the most sophisticated; and each must find their own place and make their own response. The disciplinary note, the analysis and ordering of prayer, the formal meditations and obligatory devotional rule, so characteristic of the Latin West, are hardly known in Eastern Christendom. Here the ideal of prayer is the free and secret intercourse of the soul with God; a total supernatural act achieved by many means but transcending all means, and as much within the span of the simplest as of the most instructed soul. Though here corporate worship may seem to touch the extreme of ceremonial and dramatic expression, personal worship has never lost that free spirituality and inwardness, that first-hand Evangelical quality, which is a direct heritage from the primitive Church.[13]

This combination of the corporate and the personal, this interaction of freedom and reserve, spoke to her very deeply. They corresponded to something which she saw within the tradition into which she had come.

No less remarkable are the passages where she writes of the Jesus Prayer, a way of prayer at that time scarcely known in Western Christendom, which has spread itself spontaneously through the West in the course of the last half-century.

If the simplicity of its form be disconcerting, the doctrine which underlies it is profound. Orthodoxy is penetrated by the conviction of the need and insufficiency of man, and the nearness and transforming power of God. Therefore its truest act of personal worship will be a humble and ceaseless self-opening to that divine transforming power; which enters with Christ into the natural order to restore and deify the whole world.[14]

The chapter on Anglicanism is a full and rather detailed account of its subject, which does not seek to evade its difficulties and complexity. She is clear that the Evangelical and Catholic elements both have an essential place within it. She sees as one of its outstanding characteristics its attempt to do justice both to the biblical offices of Morning and Evening Prayer and to the sacramental nature of the Eucharist itself. She tries very hard to specify what in all this development is particularly English: the love for tradition with the readiness to change; the respect for individual liberty within the framework of a common order; the desire to hold together apparent opposites in a truly balanced whole.

Within the chequered history of post-Reformation Anglicanism, it is clear that she feels a particular indebtedness to the leaders of the Oxford Movement, and amongst them not so much to the famous figure of John Henry Newman as to his less known and much misunderstood friend and colleague, Edward B. Pusey.

> Pusey, the true prophet of the movement, was by temperament an ascetic and contemplative. His inner life, disciplined by much suffering, was nourished by the writings of the great Catholic mystics, whose influence can constantly be detected in his sermons, and sometimes breaks out in passages of sustained splendour. Indeed, the modern recognition and restoration of the mystical element in religion, in so far as it is a factor in the Anglican revival, began with this scholar-saint...Those who saw Pusey in the last years of his life did not see a brilliant preacher or a determined controversialist...but a quiet man of God, inured to opposition, anxiety, failure and weariness, 'speaking in the calm power of the Holy Ghost, not as the head of a party, but as the somewhat saddened but irrepressible instrument of the Divine Will'.[15]

These last phrases come from the pen of Fr Richard Meux Benson SSJE, one of the closest of Pusey's disciples, and the most influential figure in the revival of religious and monastic communities in the Church of England in the nineteenth century. It was this revival above all else which seemed to Evelyn Underhill to be a sign of the spiritual vitality and authenticity of the Church to which she belonged:

The fullest expression of this spirit of adoration, and perhaps the greatest achievement of the Anglican revival when seen in spiritual regard, is the restoration of Religious Orders within the English Church. For the religious life sums up, and expresses in a living symbolism, the ideal consummation of all worship; the total oblation of the creature to the purposes of God.[16]

We have been looking at Evelyn Underhill's exposition of the nature of Christian prayer and worship as we find it in her major work *Worship*. We have suggested that what is particularly Anglican about the book is its willingness to be open to the activities of the Holy Spirit wherever they may be found in the Christian family and beyond it, and at the same time to locate a central core of fullness and balance in which the different elements are held together in one. Her vision is Catholic and Evangelical. Her intention is emphatically ecumenical. She sees on the one side an almost unconscious synthesis of these different elements in Eastern Orthodoxy, and on the other an almost too self-conscious effort to work towards it in Anglicanism.

Through her life and work, both scholarly and pastoral, Anglican spirituality was deepened and became more inclusive. By way of von Hügel she helped her fellow Anglicans to overcome their anti-Roman prejudices. Her contacts with Bulgakov helped her to mitigate the prevailing indifference among Anglicans to all things Orthodox. Her own explorations of the world of Nonconformity in Britain helped her to open the eyes of others to the unexpected riches to be found there. One of the distinctive marks of Anglican spirituality In the last fifty years has been precisely its willingness to learn from others, from a Russian Orthodox Metropolitan, Anthony Bloom, from a Roman Catholic monk, Thomas Merton, from a German Lutheran scholar, Dietrich Bonhoeffer. This is a quality to which Evelyn Underhill by her writings made no small contribution.[17]

III

We have spoken so far in generalisations. I want in this last section to look at one particular correspondence, hitherto unpublished, to see a little how these principles worked out in practice. The letters in question were written between 1939 and 1941 to Daphne Martin-Hurst, a woman then in her late thirties who had known Evelyn for many years, indeed since she had first gone to University in Oxford, and who had developed a deep and affectionate relationship with her. Evelyn Underhill was just the age of her own mother and she became a kind of second mother to her. They show Evelyn's way of counselling—shrewd, practical and humorous; they also show her grappling with the imperfections of the Church and the total inadequacy of language to express the mysteries of God. Here is a very practical expression of her position as an Anglican, her recognition of the presence of Christ within the imperfections and the failures of our life in space and time, her faith in a Church which is not ideal, complete or infallible, but which exists always and only from the abundant grace of God.

At the moment when the correspondence begins, Daphne is just entering the novitiate of the largest Anglican Community of Sisters. It is November 1939, just after the beginning of the second World War, and Evelyn writes to her for her clothing as Novice:

> This brings you my love and all possible blessing for your great day of self-giving. How I hope it will be full of peace and light, though even if it isn't that makes no real difference—and even gives you the chance of a *more* complete and costly sacrifice...There are bound to be some desperate moments, but abandonment can bring us safely through the very worst trials of the spiritual life. How I *wish* I could have been with you on Thursday. I shall never forget Sister Hilary Clare's clothing. It was the loveliest ceremony I have ever been at. Perhaps when you are professed things will be easier and your friends will be able to come.

The next letter comes at the beginning of February and is evidently in reply to one of Daphne's. Evelyn begins by saying that she knows that she won't hear from her during Lent, and adds, 'This letter may be on the woolly side, as I am in bed recovering from a champion attack of asthma, and not feeling very intelligent.' The handwriting certainly is not of the clearest, but the contents are sparkling. One wonders what the letter would have been like if she had been feeling intelligent.

I fancy everyone who is at all fervent suffers more or less from the shock you speak of when they come down bump onto the cocoa-nut [sic] matting of the average sister's average life. But after all a Religious Order isn't (yet) a community saints. It's a collection of people who have been given the grace to offer their lives to God—but alongside that grace, nature persists and is apt to show itself in all sorts of shabby disconcerting little ways. Still, it's part of the mystery of religion isn't it that God *does* work in the world through imperfect instruments. The Apostles themselves were in many ways a second-rate lot and *yet* they were founders of the Church. This human side of the Church has always been a trouble to keen Christians. St Teresa called the older nuns of the (unreformed) Carmelites 'the pussy-cats', and of course there is a tendency for slackness to creep into every religious order—the mere wear and tear of life tends to produce it.

After more good advice on how to negotiate the novitiate, Evelyn commends one of her favourite writers:

De Tourville, in his big book of letters, has one addressed to a novice in which he warns her especially against expecting to find the community a collection of saints, and tells her she will need the qualities of a woman of the world—tact, tolerance and commonsense—quite as much in convent as outside it!

Daphne was a woman of a keen and enquiring mind, and in a long friendship they had had many opportunities to think over and discuss the deepest questions together. Not surprisingly, she found the convent theology at time rather frustrating. This produced the most interesting of all Evelyn's letters.

I was glad to get your letter and not at all surprised that you have been having a rough time with Convent theology. There always seems to be a time-lag in religious communities. They hang on to a religious outlook which the Church outside has dropped or transformed, and continue to use the pious language of the last generation. All this presses very hardly on educated subjects and probably causes the loss of many fine vocations. But it isn't impossible if one gets *thoroughly* into one's mind the approximate and symbolic nature of all these theological conceptions—the immeasurable extent to which the mysterious realities of Christianity transcend them. Then we can just accept the particular formulas, however difficult, as part of the surroundings in which one has been placed by God, and as embodying (tho' in a manner that doesn't entirely appeal to one!) the truths by which one's soul lives. Hang on tight to what von Hügel called 'the great centralities of religion', God, Christ and the soul—and as to the rest, just let them be. Don't force yourself to swallow them and don't on the other hand let yourself be exasperated by them. Just let them alone, and remember that others' souls find food in them, even though you don't. As to the peculiar little verbal prayers I can well believe they are a trial! Anyhow they are an opportunity to mortify intellectual fastidiousness, accept the Common Life in devotion as well as in work. All that God looks for in our prayers is a movement of will and love, and this we can always offer Him, even within the silliest form of words...As far as you are able, read spiritual books of an enlarging kind, to give the mind something on which it *can* feed—St Augustine, St François de Sales, De Caussade, von Hügel.

Surely the advice being given here is not only applicable in religious communities. Much of what is said will speak directly to Christians of an enquiring mind, who may always find the formulas and conventions of their churches and congregations less than helpful. The last of the letters, written in April 1941, reflects a little of all this as Evelyn herself experienced it, increasingly hampered by the asthma which finally killed her:

I spent my Lent in one room and most of my Easter in bed! but it was very nice and peaceful. Mrs Vernon went to Tenebrae and the Ceremonies at St Augustine's Kilburn, and said it was lovely. Our very earnest though very low-church Vicar (who actually achieved a daily Mass in Holy Week) brings my Communion whenever I want. His one desire, which rather shocks my liturgical side, is that I should 'have the service just as I like it', but we are gradually teaching him!!!

What, she reflected, did the externals matter, when the heart of the matter was there; the Lord coming in the sacrament of his love.

Evelyn Underhill died on 15 June 1941 at the age of sixty-six. In the last years of her life, frequent ill-health, particularly recurrent bouts of asthma, had sometimes made her feel old beyond her years. So in a letter to C. S. Lewis in November 1938 she writes, 'It sounds as though you suspected me of being a terrestrial sorn, instead of just an elderly mouse.'[18] Her friends describe her as frail, but full of a quiet joy. There were occasions when the frailty seemed to become transparent, 'a face that could look like alabaster with a light behind it.' One such moment is recounted in Charles Williams's introduction to her *Letters*, a moment of a kind of transfiguration. It is interesting that Charles Williams ends that introduction with an evocation of the Chapel of the Retreat House at Pleshey, a place which was very dear to her and where there is now a plaque which commemorates her. It is a place which still seems to be full of her presence. Just after the dedication of the chapel Evelyn wrote to a friend, 'The new Chapel is most beautiful and simple and seems to have been born full of the spirit of prayer.'[19] That is a truth to which many have borne witness over the years. The Franciscan priest who first told me to visit Pleshey over forty year ago, said, 'The Blessed Sacrament isn't reserved in the chapel, but it feels as though it were throughout the whole house.'

The building of this chapel owed much to the vision and determination of one of Evelyn's closest friends and collaborators, Lucy Menzies, at that time Warden of the Retreat House. Before the service of dedication she had arranged for an all-night vigil of prayer. Agatha Norman, at the end of her life, confided to me that when she came down in the middle of the night to take her turn in the prayer watch, she found only two people praying there, Evelyn and Lucy. But the whole place seemed full of presences. It was for her in the silence of Pleshey, as it had been for Evelyn in that grimy Presbyterian mission hall, 'an overwhelming supernatural impression'. Here was indeed a woman in whose life God's glory was present and at work, shining out in ways that could not always be hidden. Her life, her teaching and her example, these are not dead but living things. I rejoice that the Episcopal Church of the United States has numbered her among the saints. May she aid us all by her prayers to come to that vision of the divine glory for which she sought, by which she lived. May we learn to say with her, 'Blessed be God that he is God, only and divinely like himself.'

NOTES

1   Evelyn Underhill, *Worship*, London 1936, p. 335.
2   Chief among them were Agatha Norman and Daphne Martin-Hurst. Agatha Norman came to know Evelyn Underhill very well during the 1930s, at the time when she was studying for a degree in theology at King's College, London. In Evelyn's last years she sometimes acted as her personal assistant, and would, for instance, read a lecture on her behalf when Evelyn was prevented from fulfilling an engagement by one of her attacks of asthma. She above all helped Evelyn in the formation of the prayer groups which were started in the last years of her life.

Daphne Martin-Hurst had known Evelyn since the early 1920s. After a career as an almoner, she entered the Community of St Mary the Virgin at Wantage in 1939. At that time she destroyed all Evelyn's earlier letters to her: 'Well, I thought I had better give up everything.' Fortunately, the letters written after that time were kept. Shortly after Evelyn's death Daphne had a serious breakdown in health and had to leave the community. She later resumed her work as a medical social worker and, like Agatha Norman, retained till her death in 1993 vivid memories of Evelyn Underhill, moving, perceptive and entertaining.

3 Charles Williams, ed., *The Letters of Evelyn Underhill*, London 1943, pp. 116-7.
4 Margaret Cropper, *Evelyn Underhill*, London 1958, p. 188.
5 W. R. Matthews, *Memories and Meanings*, London 1969, p. 132.
6 *Letters*, p. 207.
7 Ibid., pp. 125-6.
8 Ibid., p. 195.
9 Ibid., p. 126.
10 *Worship*, pp. xi-xii.
11 Ibid., p. 306.
12 *Letters*, p. 248.
13 *Worship*, pp. 270-1.
14 Ibid., p.274.
15 Ibid., pp. 331-3.
16 Ibid., p. 333.
17 See the article on 'Contemporary Anglican Spirituality' in *The Study of Spirituality*, ed. by C. Jones, G. Wainwright and E. Yarnold, London 1987.
18 *Letters*, pp. 269.
19 Ibid., p. 210.

The Letters

Daphne Martin-Hurst, to whom these letters were written, had known Evelyn since the early 1920s. After a career as an almoner, she entered the Community of St Mary the Virgin at Wantage in 1939. At that time she destroyed all Evelyn's earlier letters to her: 'Well, I thought I had better give up everything.' Fortunately, the letters written after that time were kept. Shortly after Evelyn's death Daphne had a serious breakdown in health and had to leave the community. She later resumed her work as a medical social worker and retained till her death in 1993 vivid memories of Evelyn Underhill, moving, perceptive and entertaining.

Highden House
Washington
Sussex
Nov. 28, 1939

My dearest Daphne,

This brings you my love and all possible blessings for your great day of self-giving. How I hope it will be full of peace and light; though even if it isn't, that makes no real difference—and even gives you the chance of a *more* complete and costly sacrifice. I never supposed you would find all this anything but hard; and the hardness must come in at so many different points and in so many subtle ways as you are steadily battered into complete surrender! But that kind of hardness, as long as it is generously accepted and never resisted, can co-exist with essential peace, can't it? and that is what I wish for you. There are bound to be some desperate moments, but abandonment can bring us safely through the very worst trials of the spiritual life. How I *wish* I could have been with you on Thursday. I shall never forget Sister Hilary Clare's clothing. It was the loveliest ceremony I have ever been at. Perhaps when you are professed things will be easier and your friends will be able to come.

You won't be able to write for a long time, I expect. But do let me know your address when you can (I take it that like most new novices you will be sent off to a branch house!)

Dearest Daphne, may your life grow steadily in depth and in joy.

Ever your affect.
Evelyn Stuart Moore

My dearest Daphne,

I was *so* pleased to get your long letter, also the previous one about De Tourville which your sister forwarded to me a few days ago. No, I know I shan't hear from you during Lent, but I'll try to write from time to time. This letter may be on the woolly side, as I am in bed recovering from a champion attack of asthma, and not feeling very intelligent.

I fancy everyone who is at all fervent suffers more or less from the shock you speak of when they come down bump on to the cocoa nut matting of the average sister's average life. But after all a Religious Order isn't (yet) a community of saints. It's a collection of people who have been given the grace to offer their lives to God—but alongside that grace, nature persists and is apt to show itself in all sorts of shabby disconcerting little ways. Still, it is part of the mystery of religion isn't it that God *does* work in the world through imperfect instruments. The apostles themselves were in many ways a 2nd rate lot and *yet* they were founders of the Church. This human side of the Church has always been a trouble to keen Christians. St Teresa called the older nuns of the (unreformed) Carmelites 'the pussy-cats': and of course there is a tendency for slackness to creep into every religious order—the mere wear and tear of life tends to produce it.

Of course I don't know how serious the things are which have upset you. I know that Hilary Clare did once come up against something she felt quite wrong, and told Mother Juliet, who was her Superior, and it was attended to. But in a general way a novice has no standing and it would be far best to avoid criticisms as far as possible. The master-word for you really is, 'What is it to thee? Follow thou me.' Your responsibility begins and ends with co-operating with the grace which has been given to you ; and the more you attend to just that and the less you judge others, the better. I am perfectly certain that all religious orders exhibit this gap and contrast between the ideal and the actual; *but* at the same time they do offer to each soul the opportunity of complete self-donation to God.

I think you could tell your novice mistress that you have been troubled about all this and ask her counsel; but it would have to be from a very humble non-assertive point of view! De Tourville in his big book of letters, has one addressed to a novice in which he warns her especially against expecting to find the community a collection of saints; and tells her she will need the qualities of a woman of the world—tact, tolerance, and common-sense—quite as much in the convent as outside it! Those whose fervour has been worn down by years of monotonous work and who have not enough spiritual vitality to make this good, have a right to our compassion—and also for our respect, for after all they *are* sticking it out as well as they can as part of the rank-and-file.

I'm so glad you liked De Tourville, and hope you will like *Abba* too when you get him back! Yes, I'm sure the entire detachment about books is a fine bit of discipline!

Your work does sound interesting. It is good to hear of such an alive parish, with every one turning up for Mass. In our poor little village we are often the only people; but Storrington, 4 miles off, has a daily Mass and is very alive.

When Audrey was here, she took me to the Convent of the Holy Rood at Findon, where I met Mother Amy, and they asked me to their festival tomorrow: but alas! I can't go. It's a lovely place, and the poor old trouts they care for seem happy.

> With much love and a blessing
> Your ever affect.
> Evelyn Stuart Moore

Highden House
March 5, 1940

My dearest Daphne—

It was such a joy to get your letter. I didn't know you had been told I was ill and felt worried not being able to write to you. Thank you *so* much for your prayers and for being remembered at Mass. This has been quite a fierce time and I shall still be some time in bed and not able to go back to London till after Easter.

I was so glad to hear from Audrey that you had been sent to Spelthorne—I had always heard it was such a good house, and that the work they did there was wonderful. Also I have a low, unmortified feeling that it's nice to think of you in the country in this lovely spring weather; and hope as the Lord has handed you out this nice respite you feel able to rejoice in it. I'm very lucky in being ill in such a lovely spot! I have a corner room with windows looking in two direction over the downs, and the sun pours in all day.

I'm so glad you got the better of your Swindon difficulties. I'm sure that is a patch—and a very important patch—which every one who attempts the Common Life has to deal with. We find poor, average, shabby disappointing human nature there as much as any where else—and it's just this we have to learn to see in the light of Charity, as God sees it. *Anyone* can see the perfect with the eyes of love—what matters is our attitude to the imperfect, don't you think? Do you remember the story of the nun who went to Father Doyle and asked for a transfer to another house, because there was a very disagreeable sister? He said, 'I quite understand! You want to go where there are *two* disagreeable sisters!'

Very much love and many blessings dearest Daphne. I hope you find Lent in religion is enlightening to the spirit and not *too* hard on the flesh.

Your affect mother, E. S. M.

Lawn House
12 Hampstead Square
N. W. 3
May 3, 1940

Dearest Daphne

I was so glad to get your letter and not at all surprised that you have been having a rough time with Convent theology. There always seems to be a time-lag in religious communities. They hang on to a religious outlook which the Church outside has dropped or transformed, and continue to use the pious language of the last generation. All this presses very hardly on educated subjects and probably causes the loss of many fine vocations. But it isn't so impossible if one gets thoroughly into one's mind the approximate and symbolic nature of all these theological conceptions—the immeasurable extent to which the mysterious realities of Christianity transcend them. Then one can just accept the particular formulas, however difficult, as part of the surroundings in which one has been placed by God, and and as embodying (tho' in a manner that does not entirely appeal to one!) the truths by which one's soul lives.

Hang on tight to what von Hügel called 'the great centralities of religion', God, Christ and the soul—and as to the rest, just let them be. *Don't* force yourself to swallow them, and don't on the other hand let yourself be exasperated by them. Just let them alone, and remember that other souls find food in them, even though you don't.

As to the peculiar little verbal prayers I can well believe they are a trial! Anyhow, they are an opportunity to mortify intellectual fastidiousness, accept the 'Common Life' in devotion as well as in work. All that God looks for in our prayer is a movement of will and love, and this we can always offer Him, even within the silliest form of words. I don't know whether you have read Abbot Chapman's *Spiritual Letters*. If so you will remember how little importance he attaches to the words of a

41

prayer. Anything will do, as long as it keeps the imagination steady and allows the will to be directed to God.

As far as you are able, read spiritual books of an enlarging kind, to give your mind something on which it *can* feed—St Augustine, St François de Sales, De Caussade, von Hügel. I don't suppose you are allowed to borrow books, but if you are I'll gladly lend you some and pay the return postage. I don't expect there is much time for reading in your present life, which sounds very full. I rather like the alternation of Chapel and kitchen and hope that like St Teresa, you 'find the Lord walking among the pots and pans'.

Audrey is looking forward to visiting you! I wish I could come too; but the hay-fever season practically means the enclosed life for me as it tickles up my asthma.

Very much love and all blessings on you
Yours aff. E. S. M.

12 Hampstead Square
N. W. 3
Jul 8, 1940

My dearest Daphne

It *was* lovely to see you, I can't tell you how much I enjoyed it. And to see you, too, so fundamentally settled (in spite, no doubt, of surface perturbations) and in your right place. I think you are one of the really fortunate ones, in being called by God to this dedicated life, shown exactly where your job lies, and relieved of the what-ought-I-to-do worry, especially in these distracted times. Don't *over*do the fervour at this stage, will you? I mean, by praying as much as ever you can, not relaxing, and so on. If you do, this will react unfavourably when the dry stage comes, as it is bound to do. Let God carry you a bit and don't wriggle in his arms in the effort to help Him along, because you *can't*. I thought you might like to have the enclosed. The drawing is by Dame Werberg, the artist nun of Stanbrook, and the paper by Maisie Spens. It is part of the Abbé Couturier's movement for Christian Unity—*first* by an interior union in prayer, and gradually working towards outward Reunion.

No, I didn't feel you had said anything about the community life which was indiscreet. I do, of course, know quite a lot about it already and anyhow should never pass on anything you said.

I have heard today that owing to the restrictions of the defence-area, Pleshey has had to give up Retreats for the present, which is very sad; but there is a hope that Miss Baines and the new Vicar and his wife may live in the house, and keep the life of the chapel going. Otherwise there is the risk that it might be used for billeting, which *would* be a disaster.

All well here. We just go on from day to day doing our little jobs. It occurred to me that perhaps you might like to have the Circular letters I send to my Prayer Group (though they are *very* elementary) so next time I write I'll send the summer one.

Very much love and all blessings on you. E.S.M.

My dearest Daphne,

I think this will just be in time to catch you before you return to Wantage. It was lovely to hear from you after you got back to Spelthorne. It did sound as though life was very busy there with ARP added to your usual work! What I meant about 'fervour' was not so much lovely feelings which soon wear off under pressure of a stiff nature and fatigue, but the fact that you *are* keen and will be naturally inclined to adopt a rule or ask for a rule which represents as much as you can do. E.g., the 5:30 rising for extra prayer, which I am so glad to hear has been stopped for the present! I know the fact that you loathe early rising must make it seem a specially excellent discipline and something worth offering to God; but really the thing *most* worth offering to God is a steady well poised mind *and* body, isn't it? Free from strain and entirely at His disposal. And this is achieved not by getting the last devotional mile out of the car, but by discovering and sticking to its economic speed—always rather *less* than you feel in your better moments you could manage, therefore something that even in your worst moments you *can* manage. You say you feel it's only wise to stick to the maximum rule of prayer and reading— but the point is, that if you are really to stick to it (which *is* most important) it mustn't be the absolutely maximum rule, but a little less, to allow for our humiliating human frailty. That was really all I meant. Novices nearly always plunge in and try to do all they possibly can, and so risk, and probably get, a bad slump. I'm specially anxious, knowing your temperament, that you shouldn't do that. It is exhausting and at that early stage interrupts rather than helps the formation of your soul. Look upon your *whole* day—chapel, work, intercourse with the sisters as well as your prayers, as a single offering of love and don't draw hard and fast distinctions between the devotional and active parts. When the

44

'mixed life' is perfectly achieved, its offering of the will is level and continuous. The effort to strike this balance is not in the least a 'pandering to self'—indeed there is very little in it to feed self-love. One's own likes and dislikes are merely ignored, and our chief guide is ordinary commonsense illuminated by faith, hope and charity.

Michael and Paul *do* sound nice cats. You will miss them when you go to Wantage. We have been rather alarmed by the new Gov't order against human food for pets and the lady who was fined £20 for giving meat to her St Bernard, as our Mickie always lives 'as the family'. However, a good deal of her nourishment, like ours, consists of offal! So we hope we shan't get into trouble. At the moment our great excitement is hens. We have 6 coming on Wednesday and my husband has been hard at work making the house and run. They are being established under my window so I hope they don't say Lauds and Prime at a very unearthly hour.

Very much love and all blessings
Your affec.
Evelyn Stuart Moore

Lawn House
12 Hampstead Square
N. W. 3
Jan. 13, 1941

My dearest Daphne—

I am so *very* grieved to hear the news of your mother's death and send you my love and deepest sympathy. The death of a parent is like nothing else in the world; it seems like the close of an epoch, the removal of something one has always accepted as a permanent factor in one's life. One of the few blanks that never get filled. I'm afraid your mother can never have recovered from the shock of your house being bombed; but how glad you will feel that you were able to go to her then and settle her near you sister for what have turned out to be the last weeks of her life. Nor can one really grieve except for oneself when any one is taken from this terrible world into the Peace of God. All the same, the loss is very hard to bear, and I am so sorry that this grief has fallen on you—even though it means one more link with the outer world broken, and so the opportunity of a more perfect self offering to God.

I expect you will have gone home but send this to the Convent, not knowing where you may be.

With much love and sympathy,
Affecty yours,
Evelyn Stuart Moore

12 Hampstead Square
N. W. 3
April 16, 1941

My dearest Daphne,

I must just send you a line to say, how deeply grieved I am for you at your Father's death—coming so soon after the parting from your mother. There is something very shattering—the sort of ending of an epoch—in this sweeping away of what has been the background of our whole lives, which makes the loss of parents unlike anything else. Even though, I can well believe you may be glad for him to be taken from what might have been a very lonely life, the blank remains. And yet too one seems to see God's action in and through this too, drawing you more entirely to Himself and His service, taking other relationships from your life—and though this is an austere, and will sometimes seem a solitary path, yet it will bring more and more peace, the more entirely He fills it with Himself; and lived as you are living it, in community—with the support of the 'Common Life' very safe and sure. You have come through it so well—I only hope the strain has not been too much physically. It will be nice if you get your rest soon and, I needn't say, a *very* great joy to see you.

I spent my Lent in one room and most of my Easter in bed! But it was very nice and peaceful. Mrs Vernon went to Tenebrae and the Ceremonies at St Augustine Kilburn and said it was lovely. Our very earnest though very low-church Vicar (who actually achieved a daily Mass in Holy Week) brings my Communion whenever I want. His one desire, which rather shocks my liturgical side, is that I should 'have the service just as I like it' but we are gradually teaching him!!!

Audrey, I think, is just going away but I'll let her have your message.

Very much love and all blessings,
Evelyn Stuart Moore

FURTHER READING

Select Bibliography

Abba, Longmans, Green and Co., 1940.
The Fruits of the Spirit, Longmans, Green and Co., 1942.
The Life of the Spirit and the Life of Today, Methuen and Co. Ltd., 1928.
The Mystery of Sacrifice, Longmans, Green and Co., 1938.
Mysticism, Oneworld, 1993.
The School of Charity, Longmans, Green and Co., 1934.
Worship, Eagle, 1991.
The Letters of Evelyn Underhill, edited by Charles Williams, Darton, Longman and Todd, 1991.

Books about Evelyn Underhill

Armstrong, Christopher, *Evelyn Underhill*, Mowbrays, 1975.
Belshaw, G.P.M., *Lent With Evelyn Underhill*, Mowbrays, 1966.
Blanch, B. and S., *Heaven a Dance, An Evelyn Underhill Anthology,* Triangle, 1992.
Brame, Grace, *The Ways of the Spirit*, Crossroad, 1990.
Cropper, Margaret, *Evelyn Underhill*, Longman, 1958.
Greene, Dana, *Evelyn Underhill, Modern Guide to the Ancient Quest for the Holy*, State University of New York Press, 1990.
_____*Evelyn Underhill, Artist of the Infinite Life,* Darton, Longman and Todd, 1991.
_____*Fragments From an Inner Life, The Notebooks of Evelyn Underhill*, Morehouse, 1993.
Oberg, Delroy, *Given to God, Daily Readings with Evelyn Underhill*, Darton, Longman and Todd, 1992.
Tastard, Terry, *The Spark in the Soul,* Paulist Press, 1990.